Stepping into the Light

A Spiritual Awakening

Gretchen Korzaan

 SALT RIVER

TUPPANY BOOKS
is an imprint of Salt River Publishing
Phoenix, Arizona
www.SaltRiverPublishing.com

TEXT © 2020 by Gretchen Korzaan
COVER © 2020 by Cynthia Spring

FIRST EDITION 2020
20 21   5 4 3 2 1   I
ISBN 978-1-946051-14-1

SR

Publisher discount at
SaltRiverPublishing.com

Contents

Stepping

into the Light

For Anthea,
In deep gratitude,
appreciation and friendship -
Much love, big hugs
and many thanks!

A xxoo

Book 1

A soul waking up

Talented, intuitive and creative artist Cynthia Spring designed the cover for *Stepping into the Light,* and it defines the essence of what the book represents.

We may believe we are standing on solid ground with our goals of life defined, but we are really standing on the shifting sands of time and space, as nothing in this creation lasts – it is constantly changing.

The only eternal and permanent essence is our soul, our life force, the Word or Shabd within that sustains our very existence.

As we seek and redefine our goals, the soul starts to feel joy within and we start realizing that we are actually spiritual beings having a human experience, and our focus starts to shift toward the inner truth rather than the outer shadow shapes of time and illusion. This transition is a time of incredible growth toward the light.

Step by step we go through the ups and downs of life, feeling our way, sinking at times only to rise again and yet we will find that we are moving ever forward toward the light and sound. We gradually start to feel freer and happier as we walk the changing corridor of our existence.

Hafiz tells us:

O what is laughter, Hafiz?
What is this precious love and laughter
budding in our hearts?
It is the glorious sound of a soul waking up.[*]

---

[*]For sources of all quotes, see "Notes on quotes, poems and stories."

What if?

We all have so many questions, and most seem to start with the expression What if...?

- What if there is a God – how do I reach Him/Her?

- What if I have to give up more than I'm willing to give?

- What if I can't figure out whether the struggle is worth it?

- What if all of my friends think I am flaky?

- What if I don't ever find out?

- What if I actually achieve God-realization – what then?

1

A peep inside

HAVE YOU EVER WONDERED what it would be like to step into the light of your soul? To feel an awakening, a freedom and a different sense of reality seeping into each waking moment?

Many people are curious and seeking answers to questions and ideas about what our purpose and goals are, why we are here in this human body, and the reasons behind our restlessness and desire to know and understand.

When we keep an open mind and start seeking, the saints and mystics tell us that the answers will come and perhaps we will gain a different perspective on life and what it means. The Beloved, the mysterious being who has always accompanied us, will give us a key to unlock the hidden mysteries so that our soul will realize its origin.

It is an incredible journey that all starts with our desire to know the truth. Hafiz gives us a glimpse:

The sun's eyes are painting fields again. Its lashes with expert strokes are sweeping across the land. A great Palette of Light has embraced this earth. Hafiz, if just a little clay and water mixed in His bowl can yield such exquisite scents – sights – music – and whirling forms – what unspeakable wonders must await with the commencement of the unfolding of the infinite number of petals that are the soul. What excitement will renew your body when we all begin to see that His Heart resides in Everything. God has a root in each act and creature that He draws His mysterious Divine Life from. His eyes are painting fields again. The Beloved with His own hands tending, raising like a precious child, Himself in you...

The saints and mystics all tell us that life does not begin with birth and end with death. The soul is an expression of infinite life. All souls are a spark of the divine essence, the love and light – call it God, the Word, the Kalma, the Shabd, the Creator. Whatever name we apply, all living beings are drops of the vast ocean of existence and so very dear to God.

The mystics say that as this journey unfolds, we will experience this truth. When we start to seek answers to our questions, doors and windows open and the heart expands. Being open to the possibilities shifts what we think we know and understand to be the truth.

Kabir gives us a glimpse of our true reality – that of soul – when he says:

The Lord is in me, and the Lord is in you,
As life is hidden in every seed.
So rubble your pride, my friend,
And look for Him within you.
When I sit in the heart of His world
A million suns blaze with light.
A burning blue sea spreads across the sky.
Life's turmoil falls quiet.
All the stains of suffering wash away.
Listen to the unstruck bells and drums!
Love is here; plunge into its rapture!
Rains pour down without water;
Rivers are streams of light.
How could I ever express
How blessed I feel
To revel in such vast ecstasy.

This is the music
Of soul and soul meeting,
Of the forgetting of all grief.
This is the music
That transcends all coming and going.

The saints and mystics tell us that spiritual teachers have been present since the beginning of the creation. Christ states that the Word was made flesh and dwelt amongst us. The mystics say it is the Lord's divine plan to have his sons and daughters here in human form to help us at our level so we can understand that we are actually spiritual beings, not just human beings.

The mystics tell us that when we are seeking the light, the Beloved himself will open all doors, for it is the Lord's love that will pull us in the right direction and show us the path that is right for us to follow.

Seeking the light is a very personal, private and intimate experience. It is a one-on-one relationship between the soul and the Creator – between the drop and the ocean. The Beloved wants the soul to grow to understand the light of its own being – thus the pull to seek and find the light.

As Maghribi states:

No one can find the way to Him
by his own strength;
Whoever walks towards Him
walks with His foot.
Until the ray of His love flashes out
to guide the soul,
It does not set out to see the love
of His face.
My heart is not shaken by the slightest
passion for Him
Until a passion flames from Him
and works upon my heart.
Since I learnt that the All-Glorious One
longs for me,
Longing for Him has not left me
for a moment.

The longing to know – to understand – and to strive to step into the light of our soul can be an incredible, life-altering experience.

The mystics reveal that this is our birthright – our heritage – to realize God even while in this human body. It is a lot to comprehend, for the mind is limited and deals more with the senses' outward and downward tendencies rather than the inward and upward focus of the soul. The mystics tell us if we stay open to the possibilities, amazing changes can take place within our being.

When one follows the guidance of a true living mystic, all the character traits of a good human being blossom within us like cream rising to the top of milk. The saints and mystics tell us that when we take the time to reflect, contemplate and be still, the closer we come to realizing that the divine presence is here with us and for us twenty-four hours of the day.

Rumi tells us:

> *There is a place where words are born*
> *of silence. Where the whispers of the heart*
> *arise.*
> *There is a place where voices sing*
> *your beauty.*
> *A place where every breath*
> *Carves your image*
> *In my soul.*

The mystics' only wish is for us to open to the beauty that is soul.

2

Awakening

Al-Ghazali says:

Man's five senses are like five doors opening on the external world, but more wonderful than these, he has a window inside himself, which opens on the inner world.

As we go through the day-to-day process of living our lives, many of us may find a restlessness, something missing we can't quite grasp. We seem to be searching for something more, something beyond what this world can offer. The mystics explain that these moments expand our awareness and help us see that we are more than this transitory human body – we are soul. S. Radhakrishnan shares:

Off and on, in some rare moments of our spiritual life, the soul becomes aware of the presence of the Divine. A strange awe and delight invade the life of the soul, and it becomes convinced of the absoluteness of the Divine, which inspires and moulds every detail of our life.

Perhaps some souls struggle with the feeling that they have little value in the eyes of God. How can the soul discern what is real and what is illusion? How can the soul believe that God's love is true? There is a very moving couplet by Ruzbihan Baqli that shows us the truth of God's love:

I saw God on the streets of the hidden with something in His hand. I said, "My Lord, what is it that you are holding?"

He said, "Your heart."

I said, "Does my heart have such a station that it lies in Your hand?"

He gazed at my heart, and it looked like something that was folded up. He smoothed and spread it out, and my heart covered the space from the Throne to the earth.

He said, "This is your heart. And it is the most vast thing in existence."

Then He took my heart to the angelic regions and I went with Him, until I reached the treasures of the hidden in the hidden.

The mystics say the soul has a value that goes far beyond what the world thinks, says or offers. For the world is transitory and subject to change. But our heart – the soul – is precious to God and he is pulling us from within, calling us back to our true home which is permanent and eternal.

The mystics encourage us to turn toward the Beloved in a quiet act of prayer, meditation or remembrance, for he sees, knows and responds. It can be a plea, a cry from the heart, a fervent desire to know the truth, or the simple act of asking for his help to understand who we really are.

Sanai has these powerful words on seeking:

Don't speak of your suffering – He is speaking.
Don't look for Him everywhere – He's looking
for you.
An ant's foot touches a leaf – He senses it.
A pebble shifts in a streambed – He knows it.
If there's a worm hidden deep in a rock,
He'll know its body, tinier than an atom,
The sound of its praise, its secret ecstasy –
All this He knows by divine knowing.
He has given the tiniest worm its food;
He has opened to you the Way of the Holy Ones.

Mother Teresa encourages us when she says:

The fruit of love is always in season – all you have to do is reach out your hand and pick it.

Mystics, poets, storytellers and teachers are there at each step for a seeker of the light. We need to turn our face toward the light and ask God to lead us to God.

The Prophet tells us to ask this way:

O God, give me light in my heart and light on my tongue and light in my hearing and light in my seeing and light in my feeling and light in every part of my body and light before me and light behind me. Give me, I beg you, light on my right hand and light on my left hand and light above me and light beneath me. O Lord, make light grow within me and give me light and illuminate me.

Our souls are awakening to the wonder of our divine nature. It is a journey of many lifetimes. The saints and mystics come to help us value this priceless gift of life – to realize that everything stems from the beloved Father. They teach us to slow down this harried pace that takes us outwards and downwards. The mystics encourage us to learn the pace at which to walk life's varied pathways. Hafiz shows us a beautiful way to move through our moments:

I do not
Want to step so quickly
Over a beautiful line on God's palm
As I move through the earth's
Marketplace
Today.
I do not
Want to touch any object in this world
Without my eyes testifying to the truth
That everything is My Beloved.
Something has happened
To my understanding of existence
That now makes my heart always full of wonder
And kindness.
I do not
Want to step so quickly
Over this sacred place on God's body
That is right beneath your
Own foot
As I
Dance with

Precious life
Today.

The mystics tell us that life is precious and precarious at the same time. Moment by moment we can grow toward the light and experience true and lasting joy for our souls, or we can step into life's shadow show and see this opportunity pass us by.

Time is fleeting and has a way of passing us by so quickly we can hardly catch our breath. That is why remembrance is so valuable to inner awakening. The saints say that each breath can be an opening for the soul.

Our spiritual teachers come to help us appreciate each moment, as nothing on this plane of existence lasts forever – it is temporary, subject to decay. They tell us that the soul never dies – it is eternal, a spark of the divine flame that is God. The Word of God is the life force that allows breath and resides in every living creature. The Lord is there for the soul each step of the way.

The science of the soul is like a laboratory within our own body, where we can actively seek and find God while living a balanced life. Our focus slowly shifts to an inner reality that is identified with the soul. The mystics tell us this is the true awakening. Rumi asks us:

Each moment from all sides rushes to us
The summons to Love.
Do you want to come with us?
This is not the time to stay at home
But to go out and give yourself to the garden.

The saints and mystics say we have had a relationship with God from the very beginning. He knows us and loves us far more than we can possibly imagine. We have had relationships for possibly thirty, forty or fifty years with our parents, our family, our friends – but the Creator has loved us from the very beginning of time. His love is unchanging and permanent.

Realizing God is the greatest gift the Lord can bestow on anyone. Is this not worth our honest efforts to seek the light? The mystics tell us the Lord's love for us is beyond imagining. This is the one love that can fill us completely, and is real, honest and lasting. Hafiz tells us:

My Beloved said, 'My name is not complete
without yours.' And I thought: How could

*a human's worth ever be such? And God,
knowing all our thoughts, and all our thoughts
are just innocent steps on the path, then
addressed my heart. God revealed a sublime
truth to the world when He sang: 'I am made
whole by your life. Each soul, each soul
completes me.'*

3

Opportunity knocks

The saints encourage us to follow the journey as it ebbs and flows and opens the heart to unveil the mysteries that currently shroud the soul. It is a process that is wondrous and terrifying at the same time. It means letting go of outer knowledge and turning inward toward the source – the eternal light.

This is possibly new ground for most of us that are seeking the light. Outer knowledge does not offer a roadmap that leads within. Only the saints and mystics can show us the way, through their own personal experience.

It does not happen all at once, as each step offers choices and destiny and dreams. But the journey itself offers the opportunity to explore, to expand our inner horizons and begin to understand that our true nature is that of spirit – soul. Hafiz tells us so beautifully:

*Picture the face of your Beloved becoming
your face, and His body fitting on you like a
coat you won't take off again.*

*Don't move so fast now, when such a rare
kiss is being offered. For what lips can really
connect with a body wired to a mind that is
darting about in a manic hurry?*

*From this new perspective, look inside the
Heart you have sought so long to be near. Try
and go deep into it. Is it not your own, and
Mine too?*

The mystics tell us that we must simply be
receptive and open ourselves to the light within.
Let go of all that is other and embrace the journey
of the soul. It is a moment-by-moment process of
shifting the attention and listening in a new way.
Mark Nepo shares:

*If I dare to hear you,
I will feel you like the sun
And grow in your direction.*

Opportunities continually present themselves to
further the growth of the soul. The mystics tell us
that each moment can expand our understanding
and awaken us to change if we fine tune our

awareness to absorb what is being offered. Charles Filmore tells us:

The abundance of life is always present. When we recognize it, it opens our consciousness... and it comes flowing in mind and body with a mighty quickening healing power that renews, transforms, and changes.

Many people find they are afraid of change and transformation; they remain comfortable in their daily routine and don't like to embrace anything different. However, there continues to be a restlessness in the soul that draws us into questioning our behavior and that creates the desire to know the deep inner meaning of life.

We struggle and we question, and if we continue to seek, the mystics tell us we will find the rewards to be great. This process of redefining who we are takes time, so we must be patient and gentle with ourselves as we grasp the deep mysteries of the soul. It is an awakening, a blossoming, an awareness that will take our breath away. As Mark Nepo puts it:

We can keep beginning, keep emptying, keep breathing ourselves open.

And we shouldn't worry about the past actions in our lives, for we only truly have the present moment, and we can start from now. This is the only moment that matters. Rumi says:

Come, come, whoever you are –
Wanderer, worshiper, lover of leaving –
What does it matter?
Ours is not a caravan of despair.
Come, even if you have broken your vows
A hundred times – Come, come again, come.

What an invitation! The mystics say our soul is hungry to know the source, to step into the light of its being, to understand the mystery called life.

One mystic shares this advice: The past is gone, it is an empty shell, let it go. The future – leave that to the Lord. The present – think positive thoughts and do positive actions.

How we think and how we act create personal experiences leading to the soul's growth. It is a slow unfolding of life's mysteries and can be very challenging.

Can we begin to grasp this at our level? No – the mystics teach that only personal experience, through our day-to-day living, will unveil the secrets that lie within. Joseph Campbell says:

> *Where you stumble and fall*
> *There you discover gold.*

The efforts we make, the joys, disappointments and struggles, transform the soul and help us understand who we truly are. Hazur Maharaj Charan Singh tell us:

> *We have no concept of the soul, and that*
> *means we have no concept of ourselves.*

To know ourselves, we need to understand that this human body is a precious gift and is meant to be used to expand our limited thinking to encompass so much more that is unlimited and waiting for our time and attention.

Mark Nepo says in his book, *The Exquisite Risk*:

> *You see, we've always been on a journey, like*
> *it or not, aware of it or not, struggling to enter*
> *and embrace things as they are... Come, there*
> *are teachers everywhere.*

Chinese wisdom tells us that the journey of a thousand miles begins with one step. A step forward to our spiritual awakening.

Shall we begin?

4

The purpose
of a human birth

This gift of a human birth: what does it mean to us during this span of time we have been granted here on earth?

If we look at things logically, we weren't able to choose our parents, our country, our gender, or the time and place of our birth. We couldn't control the conditions of our environment, our schools or city as we were growing up. Perhaps as we grew older, we protested against what we felt was wrong and rebelled against the restraints that were placed upon us. We felt we were in control of our destiny.

And, indeed, we did have choices. Life is an endless journey of discovery. As we grew, we felt all of the emotions coursing through our system: joy, surprise, achievement, doubt, frustration and love.

We possibly felt praise from our parents and guidance, but we may have also felt abuse or indifference. These moments all helped to define us outwardly as well as inwardly. The mystics tell us each step in our lives has created the veils that cover, encase, cage and keep the soul helpless and separated from its source, the divine eternal light.

This is a normal process – called growth. No one experiences only joy or only sorrow; life is a mix and a challenge. One of the secrets is to step back, slow down, take a close look at what we are feeling and what we are thinking that may influence our actions. Take the time to simply **be**.

Hazur Maharaj Charan Singh tells us:

As to intellect, God gave it to us simply to carry on our worldly work. Beyond that our wisdom does not help. God wants us to rise above cold reason on the wings of love for Him and see Him with the eye of the soul.

How we define ourselves definitely affects the choices we make each and every day. The saints and mystics explain that God wants us to go beyond the finite and see what lies beyond this world. But first we have to understand ourselves. Who are we? Rumi says:

*You are more precious than both heaven and
earth. What can I say more? You know not
your own worth. Sell not yourself at little
price, being so precious in God's eyes.*

Outwardly, we are either a man or a woman
presented in the human form. Inwardly, the
mystics say we are the essence of life itself – the
soul. Physically, the human body is comprised
of air, water, fire, earth and ether – these are the
dynamic elements that construct our outer being.
But the life force, the breath of life, comes from
the soul. So you could say we are a combination
of physical and spiritual components.

But what do we identify with – the body and the
mind, or the soul? Or all three?

An important question to ask ourselves is what
is real and lasting? What has value in our lives?
The saints say that God alone has lasting value
in our lives, and as we seek the truth we will start
to understand what this means.

Hazur Maharaj Charan Singh explains:

*Love alone is eternal and God is love. He
alone is permanent, unchanging, everlasting
on the otherwise shifting sands of time and*

space.... The very reason we are placed on this earth is to enable us to realize God within ourselves.

What a wonderful and telling statement – "The very reason we are placed on this earth is to enable us to realize God within ourselves."

Man is a sentient being – we have the power of discrimination and act according to the choices we make. While in this human body the mystics say we have the capacity to actually realize God. This is no small matter. The choices we make are very important for the growth of our soul. And it doesn't matter what other people may think, for this is a personal relationship between our soul and God.

In this wonderful poem "Anyway," written on the wall in Mother Teresa's home for children in Calcutta, it speaks about being our true selves:

People are often unreasonable, irrational and self-centered. Forgive them anyway.
If you are kind, people may accuse you of selfish, ulterior motives. Be kind anyway.
If you are successful, you will win some unfaithful friends and some genuine enemies.

Succeed anyway.

If you are honest and sincere people may deceive you. Be honest and sincere anyway.

What you spend years creating, others could destroy overnight. Create anyway.

If you find serenity and happiness, some may be jealous. Be happy anyway.

The good you do today will often be forgotten. Do good anyway.

Give the best you have, and it will never be enough. Give your best anyway.

In the final analysis, it is between you and God. It was never between you and them anyway.

So let us reflect:

We all want to be good human beings, with qualities such as kindness, compassion, understanding and good will. But beyond that, most of us are searching for something more in our lives.

There seems to be a restlessness that drives us to continue asking questions, an awareness that grows as life progresses. It nags and pulls us to continue to seek answers.

Hazur Maharaj Charan Singh says:

Man seeks the Lord because He is his origin. Life does not begin with birth and end with death. We are an expression of infinite life, which has no beginning and shall never come to an end.

This is what the mystics come to share with us.

5

What is real?

What is real? The saints and mystics say only the essence of our soul is real. Everything else perishes. Nothing in this world is lasting, except the source, the inward breath of soul.

One of the choices we make will be what we focus on in life. How we spend our time and attention can make the difference in experiencing and understanding the truth, or leaving the world as an empty, seeking shell.

There is a wonderful teaching story by Swami Chidivilasananda that explains a bit about our situation. He says:

> *A thousand mirrors were neatly placed on the table of my life. Since life itself was an enigma, I looked for meaning in the reflections.*

*Each mirror had its own width and depth and
also its own distortions. Some reflections
were smaller, and others larger; still others
were totally out of proportion, yet they
seemed to speak about life and shed meaning
on existence. I watched the myriad reflections
of feelings, thoughts, and actions.*

*In the beginning it was all fun, like a child's
game – but the game was not distant from
reality. A thousand mirrors became my
dwelling. Time passed, watching. It seemed a
comfortable way of living.*

*Then the Guru's grace struck my life. One by
one, each mirror was shattered to pieces. The
reality of my existence was at stake. The table
of my life was shaking.*

*As grace continued to strike, each mirror was
broken into thousands of fragments. The
reflections became innumerable. But now
they no longer made sense. Each single clear
reflection had become multifaceted. One
reflection of sadness became many. One
reflection of joy was also multiplied. Yet
nothing held true meaning any more.*

The Guru's grace continued to strike.
Ultimately, the last mirror, so dear to my heart,
the mirror which maintained the difference
between the individual soul and the Supreme
Soul, was about to be destroyed.

My whole being wept. My senses abandoned
me. My world crumbled. Destruction took its
time. While grace was penetrating deeply, I
said to myself, 'People say grace is a shelter.
Why, then, am I losing all I have?'

The last mirror, which gave me hope, which
gave me support, my dearest friend for
lifetime after lifetime, was about to become a
prey of grace.

The sword of light shone brilliantly; reflections
melted in this mirror. Finally, when the
strongest mirror exploded, not even a trace
remained of that existence which had once
found meaning in reflections.

A wondrous thing had happened. All the
reflections had become grace; all the mirrors
had become grace. Grace had revealed that
everything is grace.

The Guru smiled as my non-existent life
merged into one truth – the love of my Guru.
The table of my life had vanished: my life itself
had become the life of my Guru.

These are powerful and poignant words, ripe with
so much meaning. When our mirrors of illusion
are shattered, the way to true understanding is
revealed, doors of mystery are opened and we
step into a new light of being.

Rumi says:

There is a voice in all that is ever present,
a voice that always sings its melody to the
world. This is the voice of truth and certainty,
the voice that lays bare the hidden mysteries
of the soul.

The mystics say when the slate of our mirror is
wiped clean of 'I' – the persistent and crusty ego
that 'Edges God Out' – the way to God's door
expands and opens and we are simply amazed
at the wonder that lies within the center. But why
has God chosen to reveal this to our souls? The
simple answer is that He loves us completely.

6

Why me?

Hafiz has this to share with us:

*How many times do you need to hear who
you are before you begin to cash some of that
in and stop acting like a beggar... for any kind
of attention from people who do not really
love you?*

The mystics all tell us *we* are what we focus on.
The one who loves us purely and completely is
the Lord. The Lord sees our restlessness and
desire to know and experience the truth – that
we are soul. Rumi says:

*O my soul, where can I find rest but in the
shimmering love of His heart?*

The saints tell us that as we progress spiritually,
we will find the world does not satisfy us any more,
that all of the activities we used to enjoy no longer

have the same pull or meaning. We start looking for something more out of life.

When we turn within, we find a contentment and start to understand the only true rest and happiness lie in the arms of the Beloved, for we are an expression of infinite life.

Hazur Maharaj Charan Singh encourages us when he says:

> *Life does not begin with birth and end with death. We are an expression of infinite life, which has no beginning and will never come to an end.*

The mystics say they come into this creation to fill our souls with the singing, vibrating essence of the Word, the Shabd, and to show us our real selves, our divine identity – as beings of light.

The true purpose of the mystics and saints is to help souls bridge the gap between the outer and the inner. We may ask: Why do we need a guide or a teacher to find our way within? Why do we need a living master? Hazur Maharaj Charan Singh explains:

You see, the master is a medium between the soul and the Lord, and he is concerned with the soul – to help it develop to reach to the level of the Father. The soul, being in the body and being a slave of the mind, is ensnared in karmas. So it has to go through certain types of karmas – otherwise nobody can stay in a body. That is known as destiny.

Master definitely helps the soul to develop spiritually... He gives a source of strength to the soul to spiritually develop within so that it is transported to the level of the Father and gets released from the mind and thus from birth and death.

That is his duty. Our real master is Shabd (the Word), which is within every one of us, and there is nothing which is hidden from the Shabd. If He is the Creator, He is also all-pervading and all-knowing.

The Word, which created the whole creation, is the true master. And it is within every one of us. So He is the Creator; He is all-knowing, all-pervading; nothing is hidden from Him.

In the flesh, the true master has realized the Word within – and we are connected through Him to that Word.

The mystic teachings say every living being is a spark of the divine creator, a drop from His ocean of love. But only in a human form do we have the opportunity to seek and find the truth.

We all know that the world encroaches on our time and attention. It is not easy to seek enlightenment and connect to that Word of God. Commitment and focus will help us find those answers. As Hafiz challenges us:

> Not many teachers in this world can give
> you as much enlightenment in one year as
> sitting all alone for three days, in your closet,
> would do. That means not leaving. Better get
> a friend to help with a few sandwiches and
> the chamber pot. And no reading in there or
> writing poems – that would be cheating. Aim
> high – for a 360 degree detox!... A ruby is
> buried there.

Time is one of our most precious companions. We need to tend to it well and work diligently to merge into the source and be immersed in the light. Step by step, breath by breath, all will be revealed. This is the promise of the mystics. When we sincerely seek, the Lord will send one of his sons or daughters to show us the way back to God.

Yogananda asks us to

> rouse the eternal flames of divine memory
> until they burn away your forgetfulness and
> you remember that you always have been, and
> are even now, one with the Lord.

The more earnestly we seek, the more answers will be revealed and we will feel the Lord's continuous presence to a greater degree throughout our days. The abundance of the giver draws us into a close embrace and we start to know our soul more intimately. Hazur Maharaj Charan Singh states:

> If we give ourselves to the wave, the wave
> takes us back into the ocean, and we become
> part of the ocean.

We find wonderful teaching stories throughout the mystic way that help us to understand the value of this human birth. Sadi shares the story of a raindrop with us:

A raindrop fell from a spring cloud, saw the vastness of the sea for the first time, and was astounded and ashamed.

"What am I next to the sea?" it whispered to itself. "Compared to the sea I am less than nothing. I am as if I didn't exist at all."

Moved by the raindrop's self-contempt, an oyster took it into its heart and Fate so shaped its destiny that eventually the raindrop became a famous royal pearl.

It was raised up because it was humble. It knocked at the door of Annihilation and became at last alive.

Many of us may not know what we are seeking or where we are headed, but when we stay open to the possibilities, God awakens us to the reality that is soul.

This human birth is a rare and precious opportunity to seek and find and participate in the divine light. The mystics say we should not wait until after we die to find God, for He lives within our souls twenty-four hours of the day and He is waiting for us to knock on His door.

He will give us everything, if we but ask. Anything in life worth having takes effort, and that is also true of God-realization. Saint John of the Cross says beautifully:

The Exquisite Risk is to still our own house.

Stillness, contemplation, knocking on the inner door – according to the teachings of the saints this is how we will find God. Whatever might appeal to us – meditation, prayer, the quiet welcome of a church, gurdwara or synagogue – when effort is made, God will find us.

The Bible says:

Be still
And know that I am God.

Saints and mystics tell us that we are spiritual beings having a human experience. Can you imagine? We are in this human body, yet we are spiritual beings. This is where restlessness of the soul comes from. This is what causes us to seek the truth.

Hazur Maharaj Charan Singh says:

Man is essentially divine. He has within himself all of the attributes of God. He has been made in the image of the Lord. The greatest of His gifts is the Word or the Logos that lies hidden within the human body.

...The whole reason that we're in this creation is to learn how to respond and learn to love and give it back to Him.

The saints tell us love takes on a practical cloak. It can never be described; love can only be experienced – and it takes effort to learn how to respond to that love and give it back to God.

This is what remembrance is all about – whether in prayer or meditation or holding his hand throughout our daily routine in life – it is keeping him close that matters. God loves our efforts to please him. As Kabir says:

The story of Love can never be told.
It is the sherbet of the dumb man
Who eats it and smiles silently.
Without any earth and without any seed,
The tree of Divine Love just grows and grows.

Heavy with a million radiant fruits
My Lover picks for me to taste.
The story of Love can never be told.

When I calmed my mind
And entered my heart,
The Love of the Lord
Leapt like a flame within me.
All my old ideas and beliefs
Just blew away like chaff in the wind.

It wasn't because of anything I am;
It wasn't because of anything I did;
But only because of Him and His wild,
miraculous, grace
That I learned at long last the lesson of Love.
My coming and going have ended;
My mind has melted in the Mind.
Don't ask me to speak any more –
The story of Love can never be told.

All mystics tell us that love is for us to experience –
words can never explain the sweetness, the pure
depth of consciousness that enters our being
when the soul is immersed in the Lord's love. He
is the true giver, and his love for us a constant

presence in our lives: a cup of nectar that we can savor at any given moment.

Do we dare to dip our toes in the water of his love? We have absolutely nothing to lose and everything to gain by making the effort to seek the truth, to explore his love, to tap into the riches of our spiritual heritage.

This couplet by Hafiz explores the mystery of our desire to realize God:

Birds initially had no desire to fly. What really happened was this: God once sat close to them playing music. When He left they missed Him so much their great longing sprouted wings, needing to search the Sky. Listen, Hafiz knows, nothing evolves us like Love.

We are like uncut diamonds, waiting for the polishing stone of the truth to make us shine. The mystics see only the beauty of our souls – always.

7

The Word of God

The mystics teach that one of the keys to human life is to focus on the Word – the Shabd, Audible Life Stream or Sat Nam – while we have breath to do so.

In the Bible, Christ referred to the Word, the Holy Spirit, as the Voice of God. This Word is referred to as Kalma in the Koran. In Indian mystic writings the Shabd, Audible Life Stream and Sat Nam all refer to the Word, Sound or Spiritual Sound, the True Name.

When the soul manifests in the body as consciousness, the Word of God manifests itself as inner spiritual sound.

Saints tell us this Word of God sustains and maintains the entire creation – we would not exist without this life force as our pulsing breath. But how much attention do we pay to this Word, the very essence of our life? Let's explore the possibilities and dive into the true root of our being.

Richard Rolle tells us:

God cannot be conceived by the mind, but knowing Him is to love Him; loving Him is to sing in Him; singing to rest in Him, and by inward rest to come to endless rest.... If you would stand well with God, and have grace to rule your life and come to the joy of love, repeat His Name – so fasten it in your heart that it is never lost from your thought. And when you speak to Him, it shall be in your ear joy, in your mouth honey and in your heart melody.... If you think on the Name continually, and hold it firmly, it purges your sin and kindles your heart.... Think it (the Name) in your heart night and day as your special – dear treasure. Love it more than life, root it in your mind. Love Him for He made you. Give your heart to Him for it is in His debt. Therefore set your love on His Name, which is healing...

All mystics state that our whole perspective on life changes as we turn from the outer world of illusion to the inner reality of God's Name.

Contentment comes, fulfillment comes, tranquility
and peace reign supreme and we start feeling his
presence everywhere. Samarth Ramdas says:

Ceaselessly repeat the Name of God
And you'll find fulfillment.
Every day, and regularly –
Early morning, afternoon and evening –
Keep repeating the Name.
Through times of happiness or hardship,
Times auspicious or inauspicious,
Resting and sleeping, keep repeating the
Name.
Walking, talking, eating, working,
Enjoying the pleasures of life,
Never forget the Name.
Rich or poor – whatever your destiny –
Stay in the atmosphere of the Name.
In childhood and youth, in dark days and old age,
In all stages of life – and at the end –
Keep repeating the Name.
Great merit goes to those
Who live in constant meditation.
The Name destroys mountains of misdeeds,
And it's open to everyone – it knows no

High or low, intelligent or dull.
All can cross the ocean of existence
With the help of the Name, says Ramdas.

Simple? When we give our hearts to God, we will find him everywhere, in everything. Hazur Maharaj Charan Singh states:

God is in everything. God itself is reality.
Wherever God is, is a reality.

Religion is a wonderful aspect of life. It doesn't matter what denomination or sect or creed you believe in. Anything that helps turn our thoughts to God is special and valuable. The big picture is to ask ourselves what fuels our soul? Hafiz tells us:

Through the stairway of existence we have
come to God's door.
We are people who need love, because love is
the soul's life,
Love is simply creation's greatest joy.
Through the stairway of existence, O,
through the stairway of existence, Hafiz,
have you now come, have we now all come,
to the Beloved's door.

The Word of God is the greatest gift the Lord can bestow – to help us realize – to help us see – that we are spiritual beings.

Hazur Maharaj Charan Singh talks about this gift:

Nam (the priceless treasure of the Word) is the greatest of gifts with which the Supreme Lord has endowed us. It is the one gate He has provided for us to get out of the wheel of births and deaths.

We can quietly stand on the sidelines and watch as our life unfolds, or we can act and question and grow. The Lord knows that we will have ups and downs and struggles and confusion, but he will always be there to support and protect and encourage us on this journey. His love for us is unchanging.

8

Destiny

The following poignant story from the July 2014 *Spiritual Link* magazine asks an important question:

As my sister and I prepared to depart for university, we awaited with some dread the predicted lecture from our dad: the lengthy talk about honouring the family name and focusing on our studies, avoiding temptations and keeping regular hours, and above all doing our very best.

To our great surprise, on the morning of our departure for college, he simply gave us each a sealed envelope, which we were instructed not to open until we reached our university residences far from home.

Setting off on the journey naturally produced bittersweet emotions. On the one hand, leaving the comforts of home and all the guidance and love of our parents' shelter was heartbreaking. On the other hand, we were excited by the prospect of new adventures and experiences.

When I reached my college room, I was eager to open the envelope. Inside was a little card, bearing in bold letters the following five words: WHAT AM I HERE FOR? Just a simple rhetorical question. The card was to be placed on the study wall above the desk, and so it was. Job done.

Initially this seemed a very simple and straightforward thing to do. But boy, oh boy, did this card come to life!

Whenever tiredness crept in and sleep seemed preferable to studying, the card would leap into view and shock my heavy eyelids to flick back up. When worldly temptations pulled too strongly, its message revived my balance and focus. If ever morals might be about to waiver, the words it bore provided guidance.

This card acted as a parent's watchful eye, a summary of spiritual values, and an invitation to remembrance of God. In a way, it built an invisible fence of principled living around my daily college life.

Thankfully, the many years of studying were safely completed. However, the message on the card had not finished its job. As time went by and the card stayed with me, it took me into layers of spiritual searching deeper than I had been inclined to explore during my college years.

It brought on an existential questioning, and a pondering on the deeper meaning of life. This eventually led to a strengthened yearning for God, which culminated at last in initiation and receiving the great gift of Nam.

The card bearing that question, 'What am I here for?', lives nowadays beside my bed. Whenever the tendency arises to slacken on the path or be carried away by the world, that battered old piece of card jolts me back into focus.

The present Master is always encouraging us to seek more meaning in whatever we do. He also tirelessly reminds us to give real focus and attention to our meditation, rather than

*letting it become a mere ritual. In fact, we
should be attentive to whatever we are doing,
and be present and focused in the moment.*

*Somehow, the card my father gave me still
serves to reinforce this message from the
Master. 'What am I here for?' is the ultimate
question for all of us. Musing upon it helps
us identify our priorities and focus on what is
most important to us. It makes us aware of
the fleetingness of time and of the things in
our lives that can steal our time. In this way, it
helps us adjust our daily schedule around our
realigned priorities.*

*Ultimately, it enables us to bring more
alertness to our meditation and to carry that
love and light into our daily life. As Guru
Arjan Dev says: 'He who cherishes the Word
within his heart, the greatest king is he; he
who has Nam within his heart will fulfil the
purpose of his life.'*

The saints say it is our responsibility to seek, to
ask questions, to study and to open ourselves to
the possibilities that will nourish our souls. This
is our true destiny. This is our real life's work
and focus.

Hazur Maharaj Charan Singh says:

What is destiny? Destiny is something with which we are born and which we have to face during our life span.... We are reaping what we have sown, and we also have the option of sowing for the future.

The mystics explain that we create karma through the actions and choices we make. Karma, to put it as Christ taught, is to reap what we sow. Action creates reaction, and each of our actions reflects on our soul, becoming part of our destiny.

Hazur Maharaj Ji continues:

Whatever we have sown in the past, we have come now to reap that portion allotted to this life. Whatever we cannot go through from what we have sown in the past is thrown into our reserve or store of karmas. So the portion allotted to this life has now become our fate karma. That is our destiny. We have to go through it.

One mystic has said that our karmic destiny brings us to a point of choice. Our destiny perhaps brings us up six flights of stairs to the top of a building. We can choose either to jump off the building or go back down the stairs. The choice we make has unavoidable consequences, now and in the future. And we never know whether we are creating new karmas or possibly eliminating the old karmas. So every thought and action is worth deliberate consideration... Every action has a consequence.

Sometimes it is easy to feel discouraged and frustrated as we go through the constant flow of our karmic destiny. We may even begin to doubt the direction our thoughts are taking us. But if we continue to make the effort, the mystics reassure us that the light within is always shining.

The mystics tell us there is a solution to everything – we should never feel discouraged. Great Master Sawan Singh encourages us when he states:

There is nothing to feel disheartened about. We are up against mind, the mind that keeps all souls out of the focus.... It is the veil that hangs between our soul and the Creator.

9

Acceptance and trust

For the seeker, the saints tell us acceptance becomes the touchstone to understanding and feeling the Lord's presence in our lives more and more.

Soami Ji of Agra – Seth Shiv Dayal Singh – tells us that

> *those who accept his word as a
> divine command are blessed with his
> companionship.*

The Great Master Sawan Singh used to tell this beautiful story:

> *There were many prisoners in a prison. It was
> summer, and very hot. The prisoners had no
> cold water to drink. So a philanthropist spent
> money to give them sweet cold drinks.*

Another philanthropist thought that they were not getting enough good food. So he spent still more money and gave them delicacies and sweet dishes. He was also doing his best to improve the lot of the prisoners.

And the third philanthropist had even more money. Winter was approaching and it was very, very cold. He gave the prisoners woolen clothes.

So each philanthropist tried to do his best to improve the prisoners' lot. But with all their philanthropy, with all their help and social reforms, the prisoners were still imprisoned in their cells. They couldn't get out. They were still miserable; only their standard of living had risen. From class C they had become class A prisoners. But all the same, they were still prisoners.

Finally a fourth person came who had the key to the prison. He opened the door and set them free.

That is the purpose of the mystic. He comes with the key to this prison – and his key is the Spirit, the Word, that God has kept within every one of us.

Now we find that besides acceptance, we need to open the heart to trust. The mystics say trust is what will lead us to that full acceptance and deep understanding of who we truly are. Our actions will slowly bridge the gap between worldly attention and spiritual intention. We will be making progress towards the light with each step we take.

From *Hunger of the Soul: A Spiritual Diary*, we read:

Then afterwards, during the question period, Swami began to talk as though he, too, had heard my begging. He looked right at me, and he said, as near as I can remember, 'You must not get discouraged if you seem not to be making progress. Every time you say the name of God with earnest intention, you have taken a great stride toward Him. You yourself cannot tell how great. Only God knows the progress you are making.

There are two things absolutely necessary in spiritual life – patience and perseverance. Be patient, persevere, meditate, meditate, and at some moment, when you least expect it, He will take you completely. Then no more doubts, no more discouragement, no more fears.

The mystics often tell us the Lord is waiting with open arms to welcome us home. When we start to step into the light, they are more anxious than we to see us face in the right direction and are overjoyed with our seeking. The mystic's presence is always there to guide and help us every step of the way – for we are part and particle of God.

Hazur Maharaj Charan Singh tells us:

> *The one who brings the soul into contact with the Shabd (the Word) is the master. He bears the same relation to the Lord as do the waves to the sea. The masters are the messengers of God who have sprung from Him, live by Him, and return to Him.*

The mystics tell us that our souls are drops of the vast ocean of God, and that we are not separate from his real form. We simply need to grow consciously to experience that oneness. Every action we take, every prayer or meditation, every effort will lead us closer to the realization that we are not separate from God. Each soul drop is part of the vast ocean of his love.

The Great Master, Sawan Singh, also explains to us that as one contemplates a being who is fearless, we become like that being.

If one wishes to become fearless one should worship the Lord. As one thinks, so he becomes. The worship of the fearless One makes you fearless also. The Lord is immanent or dwelling within you.

And Saint Kabir, one of the great Indian mystics, says:

Kabir, after careful thought, O seekers! remember the fact that when there is realization, there is no fear.

One of the main goals in following the path that calls to us is unlocking all of the doors that block us from the inner truth and light. Slowly we begin to realize we are spiritual beings in this human body. The saints tell us this is our heritage and our destiny. We find the more effort we make, the more grace we receive, and the more we grow in understanding. This is the circle of love.

The mystics share that when we act with patience, perseverance, acceptance and trust, our hearts will open to the journey within. Understanding will blossom as long as we continue to take action and keep trying.

Another way to look at it: when we are immersed in our ego, we are not open to the truth within. We are literally E – edging G – God O – out.

In "The Power of Love," an article written for *Spiritual Link* magazine, it says:

> *If one thinks of the way things work in the world, of how complex our environment is, and how many different forces are at work, one has to ask: can I as an individual take credit for anything at all?*

> *Looking at the bigger picture to the extent that we are able, we can easily see that the complexities of life make the outcome of our efforts unpredictable at best....*

> *It is not possible for us to consciously submit our will, to eliminate our ego; it is simply not in our capability. But in the state of love these things occur automatically.*

> *So perhaps we should abandon our efforts to eliminate our egos and...instead we should focus on what will create that love within us and release that latent power within us....*

*Life sometimes really seems to be like a
carpet that is rolling out in front of us and
rolling up behind us. Past and future have
an almost perceptible unreality about them,
which should leave us with questions about
the 'reality' of the present – the present which
seems so tangible and undeniable that we
tend to believe in it.*

It is difficult to understand unreality at our level,
for we are in this human form, where touch, sight,
sound and feeling play such strong roles. We touch
something and it seems to have substance; we
hear music or someone voices an opinion and it
all sounds real to us; we see many objects with
these outer eyes and possibly believe this is all
there is to see.

Our own thoughts tend to build windows and
walls, forming judgments and barriers to inner
growth.

The mystics say there is so much more for our
soul to experience. Eckhart Tolle, in a book called
Stillness Speaks, has this to share:

Most people spend their entire lives imprisoned within the confines of their own thoughts. They never go beyond a narrow, mind-made, personalized sense of self that is conditioned by the past.

In you, as in each human being, there is a dimension of consciousness far deeper than thought. It is the very essence of who you are. We may call it presence, awareness, the unconditional consciousness. In the ancient teachings it is the Christ within, or your Buddha nature, or the Shabd.

Finding that dimension frees you and the world from the suffering you inflict on yourself and others when the mind-made 'little me' is all you know and runs your life. Love, joy, creative expansion and lasting inner peace cannot come into your life except through that unconditioned dimension of consciousness.

If you can recognize, even occasionally, the thoughts that go through your head as simply thoughts, if you can witness your own mental-emotional reactive patterns as they happen, then that dimension is already emerging in you as the awareness in which thoughts and emotions happen – the timeless inner space in which the content of your life unfolds.

The stream of thinking has enormous momentum that can easily drag you along with it. Every thought pretends that it matters so much. It wants to draw your attention in completely.

Here is a new spiritual practice for you: Don't take your thoughts too seriously.

10

Who are we?

Hazur Maharaj Charan Singh emphasizes:

In spite of our eyes we are blind. We do not see the priceless treasures that lie hidden within our body.

We don't want to compartmentalize and limit the deeper truth the mystics share – we need to expand our inner horizons so we experience the truth and understand at the highest level that we are soul.

Universal Truth is at the heart of all religions and spiritual teachings. The mystics come down from their level to help bring us up to their level. The mystics see beauty in all of us, and they understand the hunger of our souls.

Thomas Merton has written:

*The path to awakening is a great and
wondrous legacy of being human. It will be
difficult and at times almost impossible.*

The mystics explain that what makes stepping
into the light a struggle is that our ego thinks
of ourselves as being separate from God, the
source of divine light. Hazur Maharaj Charan
Singh tells us:

*God is in everything. God itself is reality.
Wherever God is, is a reality.*

*The man in whom the Word of God dwells is
made like God – nay, becomes God himself.
God and the Word and the living master are
then one and the same.*

A question was asked Hazur Maharaj Charan
Singh:

*Why is a master more than a priest or a
preacher? Why is he more valuable to one
seeking spiritual salvation?*

And the master replied:

*In the beginning we should just take him as a
preacher or teacher or a guide. And when we*

go in, we will realize what he does for us. We automatically see what he is....

You see, everywhere, in every line, we need a teacher. You want to do law, you want to do engineering, we have so many teachers to put us on the path. And we always give them due respect and are grateful to them for being so helpful to us....

In the same way, we need a master, we need a guide, to put us on this spiritual path, to lead and guide us on that path. And when we realize what the path is, what the beauty of that realization is, we automatically know what we have to be, how we have to be with him.... All this comes from within.... The realization is within.

The master not only describes it to us, he actually leads us inside, and ultimately we merge back into him and he merges back into the Lord. We all become one. Everybody is a wave of that ocean.

The mystic teachings may remind us we think too little of the truth that lies within. Perhaps we feel we are not worthy to step into the light. We can see our weaknesses and faults and struggle with the idea that God could actually love us and forgive us for our shortcomings. Sarmad says:

At the dining table of mercy, Thou has been treating me like an honoured guest and urging me to take many helpings of Thy mercy. I tried to outdistance Thy grace by my transgressions, but I stand defeated; Thy generosity perplexes me.

When we shift the focus away from the world and its objects, the saints say we will start to clearly see that there is much more to experience within. And as we let go of the ego that keeps us separated from God, we will find there is no separation at all – just the merging into the ocean of his love. God loves us just as we are – for the saints tell us that he sees our possibilities.

From the *Book of Mirdad* we get this glimpse:

The Word is the ocean – you the cloud. And is a cloud a cloud save for the ocean it contains? A god-bearing cloud is man.... Except it die (and lose itself) and vanish as a cloud, it cannot find the ocean in itself which is its only self. Save he is emptied of himself, he cannot find himself.

Mirdad is talking about open secrets – the inner truth of our being – that we are not separate from God. We are part and parcel of the divine creator. He the ocean and we the drop. The saints and mystics tell us that we are all seeking the water of life, the nectar that nourishes our hungry souls.

Somewhere, a part of us realizes that the soul is eternal – much more than this quick stopover called life leads us to believe. Hazur Maharaj Charan Singh says:

Life does not begin with birth and end with death. We are an expression of infinite life, which has no beginning and shall never come to an end.

When we look at life from the perspective of the mystics, then we begin to realize that our true and lasting relationship is with the Lord.

The saints remind us how very important it is to form a relationship with the Lord, the Creator. The Creator has been with all of us since the beginning – why not develop a relationship that is lasting? Permanent? Why not attach yourself to the Creator?

We form all of these attachments for twenty, thirty or forty years with our family and spouses, relatives and friends – but the Creator has loved us from the very beginning. Why not form a relationship with him and feel his love?

There is a beautiful couplet by Yogananda that states:

The greatest romance is with the Infinite. You have no idea how beautiful life can be. When you suddenly find God everywhere, when He comes and talks to you and guides you, the romance of divine love has begun.

When we turn to the Beloved in all aspects of life, we find that his presence and grace cut through the mind's wanderings and help us focus on what is real and permanent in our lives – our soul. The mystics say our perspective starts to change and time takes on a new meaning.

Soami Ji tells us in *Sar Bachan Poetry*:

I have enshrined my Master's lotus feet within, crushing the dark tendencies of the mind. The Master has cast his merciful glance on me and shattered the wheel of time forever.

Beautiful words – our roots in this illusory creation have been cut. The wheel of time, our coming and going, birth after birth, has been shattered and there remains only the refuge and shelter of the Beloved.

There is an insightful Sufi teaching story in *Perfume of the Desert* by Andrew Harvey:

An Emperor had a slave whom he loved immensely and he wanted to know if the slave really loved him. So, into a room heaped with treasures of all kinds, with jewels and deeds to vast estates, he summoned all of his slaves and said to them 'You are free. Whatever you want in this room, you can take.'

The slaves could hardly believe their luck. They ran about trying to cram as much as what was in the room into their pockets, and then scampered out of the room, yowling, hollering and clapping their hands.

But the slave whom the emperor loved did not move from where he was standing. When the room was empty, the slave walked quietly over to the emperor and stood by him, his eyes full of love. The emperor said to him, 'What do you want?' And the slave said, 'I want you,

just you,' And the emperor said to the slave,
'Because all you want is me, all that I possess
is yours.'

Here we are talking about the relationship between the soul and the Lord – building that relationship with the Beloved in each of our worldly moments. Let's look at a few examples.

Brother Lawrence practiced the presence of God in everything he did. All of his mundane tasks were conducted in a state of constant communication with God, and he felt God's continuous presence through that constant remembrance.

Shraddha, a Catholic nun who describes her journey into truth in the book *Adventure of Faith,* says:

What wouldn't I, and hundreds of thousands
of human beings who have lived during the
two thousand years since Christ's death, have
given to meet him, to behold his face?...

Is not our longing to see God in human form
legitimate? We are accustomed to perceive
things with our senses. To this natural need
God responded by manifesting himself in the

form of the Word made flesh in Jesus Christ,
as the Gospels tell us.

But did God reveal himself in human form
only once in the course of human history? Did
he show himself to a small privileged group
on just one occasion and never again?...

My own experience had now convinced me
that God, in his loving mercy, sends his Son
into the world in human form again and again.
I was filled with indescribable joy when I
realized that even today we can behold his
face in a true living Master, a Christ. I could
never have dreamt that the words, 'Let me
behold your face' would be fulfilled in this way.

Guru Ram Das (1534–1581), one of the great
mystics of India, tells us:

My mind is restless because I do not behold
God,
Like a man dying of thirst is restless without water.
My mind was pierced by the arrow of thy
Name,
And no one dwells in my heart but the Lord.

When we are seeking the truth, wanting to step into the inner light, the mystics tell us the Lord definitely will respond. His love for the soul is pure and perfect, unspoiled and lasting. But it is our job to ask for His help and guidance. This opens the heart and mind and allows us to become more receptive to His wishes for our soul and we will start to feel the immensity of his Grace. This will nourish the flame of our longing and encourage us to continue to seek the truth.

Remember that wonderful song:

Seek and ye shall find, Knock and the door shall open, ask and it shall be given...

We must believe that it can happen, that it will happen and it is going to happen. If we just ask honestly and sincerely and keep knocking at his door, the mystics tell us the Lord is more anxious than we are to open to us – more anxious to give than we are to receive.

To feel comfortable receiving, we simply need answers to our questions and allow time for the trust to build. Hazur Maharaj Charan Singh reminds us:

Please remember that great things are not accomplished quickly. They require time and effort to achieve them.

We have to pay the price for everything. Are we ready to pay the price required for God-realization? No price is too much for this great boon.

11

Renewal

The saints teach that changes will take place as we are living in this world and seeking the inner path. The world and its attachments do not pull us like they once did. This can be a difficult time for some of us. As we become more and more detached from the world, we perhaps feel at loose ends. We may not feel totally connected outside or inside. Should we renounce the world?

Great Master Sawan Singh tells us the difference between detachment and renunciation:

When intense love is awakened, all worldly desires are obliterated and one automatically becomes detached from the world and everything in it...

So in seeking the One, the filters of the world go into the background and intense love is awakened which detaches us from worldly desires. The word

Great Master uses is 'obliterated'. The dictionary defines this as wiped out, indistinct, destroy utterly, annihilate, demolish, eliminate – well, you get the picture. Detachment from the world and its objects will completely change our lives.

Great Master continues:

No desire remains for anything in this world or the next. In this state, when the mind is free from all these desires and longs to meet the Master, the longing and the love thus created is called detachment.

In such a state, all attachment for the world vanishes, and the mind has an urge to be with the lovers of God and away from the world. A detached person is indifferent to every non-essential object of the world and runs only after his Beloved, who is the Almighty Father...

We might say, do we have to give up worldly life completely – letting go of our attachment to the world and its objects?

...True detachment consists in accepting the material comforts as well as the necessities of life merely to the extent of their usefulness for life, while realizing them to be only the means

and not the goal. A truly detached person lives in this world but does not become entangled in it. He does not consider it necessary to leave the world in order to rise above it. He sees the presence of God in everything....

Detachment is absolutely necessary in order to achieve spirituality. A seeker becomes eligible for true detachment by meeting a Master and by devotion to him. It is not necessary for him to leave his hearth and home. He becomes detached when he tastes the elixir of the soul's love.

12

Practicing the presence

The mystics and saints have spoken about the purpose of this human birth and have defined who we are in essence – soul. Now let us explore the necessity of a living teacher, someone who is at our level in the human form to help and guide us on this spiritual quest.

We need a living teacher in every walk of life, whether throughout our school years, during professional training, or parents guiding us as we grew up. In matters of spirituality, mystics tell us a living master is a vital necessity – to help us grow to understand the truth that lies within.

Great Master Sawan Singh states:

In the beginning, you are aware of Him and He of you. And then in the second state, you become His and He becomes yours. And then

in the final state you cease to exist, and He
alone fills you.

We may not realize at our level of understanding,
but our soul is an open cup, the mystics say, one
that is already filled to capacity. They tell us we
must grow to understand what this means to our
soul, so that we can feel the Lord's love fully in
our lives.

Meister Eckhart says:

It is one flash, the being ready and the pouring
in... God dispenses His Grace the instant the
spirit is ready – God enters without hesitation
or delay. You need not seek Him here or there.
He is no farther off than at the door of your
heart; there He stands lingering, awaiting,
whoever is ready to open and let Him in...

Baba Jaimal Singh tells us in *Spiritual Letters*:

If after being born in a human body one
meets a perfect Satguru, then everything is
accomplished. This is the fruit.

The saints tell us our spiritual journey is a path,
not of information, but of transformation. It is
not a path of knowing, it is a path of becoming.

It is recognizing the essential and incredible fact that we are spiritual beings, not merely physical beings. This human birth is such an invaluable gift, and we begin to see our real essence as that of soul. We start to appreciate what the mystics do for us each moment of our lives.

Great Master Sawan Singh says:

The Master stills the mind and the senses of the disciple and purifies him.... While the Master in his mercy lends help to still the mind of the disciple, he at the same time enables him to understand and to speak that language which is unspoken.

The Master is always careful about the progress of the disciple. He does everything possible to make a disciple clean, devoid of all dirt, and pure. He removes all his defects....

Maulana Rum says that we should sit at the feet of a person who knows our heart, who can understand our difficulties and sufferings, who can share our sadness and who can remove it. We should sit in the shade of a tree bearing fresh flowers and fruit, which will refresh our mind and heart, and from which we will get the fruit of spiritual life to eat.

There is contentment in knowing who we are and where we belong. When we sit in the shade of his truth, we become saturated with that divine presence and we will feel the richness of our spiritual heritage enfold us.

The saints and mystics come to our level to help us remember that we are soul. Rumi says:

Remember the deep root of your being, the presence of your Lord. Give your life to the One who already owns your breaths and your moments.

It is a burning of the heart that I want, it is this burning that is everything, more precious than the empire of the world, because it calls God secretly in the night.

We will find that all saints and mystics share the same message as we continue our journey. They want us to realize and understand that we are so much more than this human body. Hafiz says:

I wish I could show you, when you are lonely or in darkness, the astonishing Light of your own Being.

13

The magic of a mystic

The mystics tell us that they come for just one purpose, to awaken us to the light of our own being. They help us realize that our souls are part and particle of the divine essence of God, that we are not separate beings but a drop of the ocean of his love and light.

But how do we find a living master, a pure teacher of the Word, a being who is here in the human form, but is also a God-realized soul who knows the way and has the power to initiate souls into the Word, the Shabd? A mystic who has the ability to show us the way to our true inner home?

The simple truth is, the mystics say, if we seek, if we are sincere, it is God who finds us and promises to take us home.

Rumi encourages us to keep striving and seeking the light:

O weary heart, the cure has finally come.
Draw in a sweet breath for the eternal
moment has finally come. The Beloved
appears for the sake of His lovers – here in a
human form, He has finally come.

In every walk of life, we need a living guide to show us the way. It started with our parents, again with our teachers, and in whatever profession we chose, we needed someone who had knowledge, skill and the ability to take us to our highest level. We can look at the Olympic champions and their trainers as an example.

The saints tell us the mind is limited to its own realm of understanding and experience. We simply don't have the capacity to attain spiritual realization on our own. We can study, we can learn and grow to a certain extent, but to fully realize God who is unlimited?

Knowing how limited our mind is should never discourage us. For the mystics are here to show us the way, each and every step, twenty-four hours of the day, with every breath we take. Great Master Sawan Singh beautifully states:

Your face is towards the light. Let nothing
hinder or discourage you. You shall drink

*of the living waters and be thirsty no more.
No matter what may be your difficulties or
deficiencies, they shall all be overcome and
the divine shabd, whose music never ceases
within you, shall sooner or later bear you
upon its loving waves back to your original
home. Have no fear or doubt.*

Mansur says:

*Life created out of intense love is here. Come
whoever wants to get it!*

Research, study, read, and open yourself to the
possibilities. The mystics tell us not to limit
ourselves. This journey may be beyond the mind's
grasp, but not beyond the soul's attainment. When
we follow a spiritual guide, we are putting love
into action. It is an outpouring of our spirit and
heart and mind in the direction of the Beloved.

14

Practice makes perfect

Spirituality really is a very simple thing, and subsequently both surrender and submission are very simple concepts. They mean to accept, let go and let God.... Deep surrender to our lives is a profound space of acceptance. We stop putting our filter of what we want into life, and we fully accept what is. This is amazing, because it can transform our lives almost instantaneously.... You see what things really are the more you surrender your ideas about what you want. A lot of things can flow to you when you surrender to the reality that is actually before you. And surrender isn't passive. You can see where you need to take action.

The mystics tell us we must have faith in ourselves, that we can do it, we must do it and we are going to do it.

With the grace and guidance of a spiritual teacher, the way will open before us.

We go to church, a temple or satsang for inspiration and to hear teachings about the Lord. The Indian term *satsang* means company of the truth. Every path revolves around the teachings of a mystic or saint to help guide us. Here is what one mystic tells us about satsang or a spiritual discourse:

> *The real meaning of the word **satsang** is company of the truth. So wherever we meet in the name of the Father, wherever the Lord is discussed, wherever we fill each other with His love and devotion, strengthening our faith to worship Him, I think that is satsang. Because naturally in our conversation, our Master is there, Lord is there. Without that, satsang means nothing.*
>
> *We always discuss the teachings, whether he's physically present or not; but naturally, when he's being discussed, he's very much present there. He's very much alive when we're discussing his teachings and the way he has told us to lead our life.*
>
> *And when it increases our love and devotion for our Master, for the Father, then we*

become a source of encouragement and strength for each other in satsang. So as long as the Father is there, the Lord and Master is there – that is satsang.

Whether you read from the text, whether you discuss, whether you just have a conversation about him, whatever helps to develop these things – that is satsang....

If there are five, ten people, few people, a very small group – even without the text, without any book, if they discuss the teachings, they discuss the Master, they discuss the Lord, they are creating faith in each other, love and devotion in each other for the Father.

Throughout our days and moments, our thoughts can turn to the Father in appreciation and gratitude and inner prayer.

It doesn't matter whether we are at work, in the garden or in the kitchen – the mystics say it is the intention, focus and remembrance that will shut the outer doors and bring the intimacy of the Lord close to our hearts in satsang.

Great Master Sawan Singh tells us that prayer or meditation, on the other hand, require solitude:

*In order to pray correctly, it is necessary that
we should go inside and shut the outer doors,
withdraw our attention from the body, and
direct it to the feet of the Beloved. In this
sacred place, pray....*

*To lose oneself in the remembrance of the
Lord, with inner purity and sincere feelings,
is true prayer. If a prayer is made with true
inner feelings, then the all-powerful Lord
listens and invaluable benefits accrue from
His mercy.*

The mystics place great value on meditation,
remembrance and prayer for this is the time
of communion with the Lord. It is a personal,
intimate and magical sharing that no words can
describe. It is a love play between the Beloved and
the soul. It is a dance of love that completes and
nourishes and enriches our being on every level.

In her book, *Adventure of Faith,* Shraddha Liertz
states:

*The time of meditation is the most precious
time of the day for the disciple – even if
he is not always aware of it, because, as
a gift of grace, it awakens the love within
us and makes it grow. It is the time that a*

94

disciple spends with his Master or, at least, in awaiting his coming.... We should give ourselves entirely to the impulse of love and unconditional, single-minded devotion to the pure essence of God.

15

The gift of his grace

The more we seek, explore and dive into this journey, we start to realize we don't have all the answers. We struggle and don't always make the right choices. Sometimes we don't even know where to turn in our search for the truth. Our limited minds can't seem to grasp the immensity of what lies within our soul.

We must remember, at these times of discouragement, that the mystics and saints come to shower us with mercy and grace and to show us the way to the inner realms. We may not begin to grasp what this means to the soul at our level of understanding, but the saints and mystics always encourage us to continue the journey. They provide the soul with the strength and courage to explore and grow. This brings incredible joy. Sarmad shares:

*In life's experience of varied kinds – this I
have seen. Thy Grace far outweighs my sins,
dark and ugly. Strange, far from bringing on
me punishment for trespassing, they have
become an excuse for the exercise of Thy
Boundless Mercy.*

Saints tell us the choices we make, the steps we
take, are all precious to God, and when we turn
in His direction, He will respond. We may feel
this in many subtle ways, intuitively or simply
sensing his presence, guiding and helping and
supporting us throughout our days.

Bhai Gurdas encourages us:

*If you take one step to take refuge in the
Master, the Master meets you on the way by
taking hundreds of steps. If you remember
the Master just once, the Master remembers
you again and again – even if your devotion
is as small as a fragment of a cowrie shell,
the Master showers all benefits on you. The
Master is all-merciful, His praise is beyond
understanding; I bow again and again to the
one and incomprehensible Master.*

To begin each day with the mystics' promise that
the Lord has nothing but our best interest at

heart becomes a joy for our souls. To develop a routine that includes remembrance, meditation and prayer gradually will help us redirect our lives so that we continuously seek the deep root of our being. Time definitely well spent. We will begin to feel his love and presence throughout our moments, and our balance and contentment will grow.

Brother Lawrence says:

> In the beginning we have to make an effort to renounce ourselves, but after that there is no longer anything but unutterable contentment. When we face our difficulties, we have only to run back to the Lord and ask Him for His grace. When He grants it, everything becomes easy...

The mystics tell us the secret is to take refuge – seek sanctuary within his love. In a beautiful discourse several years ago at the Dera near Beas, Punjab, the speaker said we are constantly running out into the world. We sit on the Lord's lap and enjoy his presence but then we have a desire to see something that entices us and we jump off of his lap and run toward those objects. Then we get scared or frustrated and we run back to the Father's lap, where we feel safe and protected.

We keep doing this, jumping off toward the world and its allure then running back to the one who can really fill us up, the Father. Eventually when we reach his lap, all we will want to do is simply stay. Rumi says:

The earth and sky will open your purse for you and your life will change, if with all your heart you say these words each day, 'Teach me, dear God, all that you know.' One night I walked through the street feeling desperate, needing alchemy. A hooded priest passed by where there were no lamps. I could not see his face, I only heard these words that he kept repeating: 'Teach me, dear Lord, all that you know.' I knew a treasure had entered my soul.

Our personal conversations with God unveil the mysteries of both the outer creation and the inner sanctuary. The mystics state that when we open ourselves to God's presence and realize that we are spiritual beings, we will feel his love fill us completely. Our consciousness expands and we start to see just what the Lord does for us and how much he loves us.

Maharaj Charan Singh, paraphrasing the words of Jesus, shares so beautifully:

I have filled my disciples with love and devotion for You. They had forgotten You by being in love with the perishable world, but now I have turned their faces towards You. I have finished the work You gave me to do. They were Yours to begin with before the creation, but then they became lost in this world and You gave them to me to lead them back to You. Not a single one of those whom You gave to me has been lost. As You have loved me, so I have loved them.

16

Fulfillment

The saints tell us we will slowly begin to understand that life is unfolding in perfect harmony for the soul. The mystics say that everything that happens throughout our lives can bring us to the realization we are part of the divine. They tell us that the Lord wants us to grasp what this means, so we can understand, consciously, that the soul is not separate but one with the Creator. This can be accomplished now, while in this human body. Our effort and his grace go hand in hand.

Rumi tells us:

It is your destiny to see as God sees, to know as God knows, to feel as God feels. How is this possible? How? Because divine love cannot defy its very self. Divine love will be eternally true to its own being, and its being is giving all it can, at the perfect moment. And the greatest gift God can give is His *own experience. Every object, every creature, every man, woman and child has a soul and it is the destiny of all to **be** as God is.*

There are times when we may feel lost or lonely, and we don't know where to turn while seeking the light within. Sometimes we step away from the path for a while, struggling to understand why we are so restless and dissatisfied with life, or why our friends question our seeking. The mystics encourage us to remember that we are not alone, for God's love is beyond worldly concepts and illusions. He is there for us always – in all ways. He is our only true friend and loves us completely.

The Adi Granth encourages us with these beautiful words:

When an overwhelming adversity besets your path, when there is no other help, when foes hotly pursue you, when close relations desert you, when all hopes are dashed and when all avenues are closed, if you still remember God, no harm shall ever touch you.

When we put in the effort to try to understand what the mystics and saints are sharing with us, our worldly burdens may feel lighter, for the Lord is sharing them with us, and we may even feel his helping hand and his support. Can we imagine what grace he gives us to continue to make an effort day by day, week by week, year by year?

To gradually shift our focus away from this transitory world and step into the light of truth is no small matter. If this is his wish, the saints say, nothing can hold us back. Hafiz says:

> *In the morning when I began to wake, it happened again – that feeling that You, Beloved, had stood over me all night keeping watch; that feeling that as soon as I began to stir, You put Your lips on my forehead and lit a Holy Lamp inside my heart.*

The Lord loves us, The Lord loves us, the Lord loves us. The saints say all we need to remember is that the Beloved is constantly present in every breath we take. We can always run into the shelter of his grace. Our Beloved will be waiting with open arms twenty-four hours of the day, seven days of the week.

An article in *RS Greetings Magazine* says:

> *When the Master finds us, we are blind to the truth. We are suffering from the severe complications of the mind and the senses.*

*Our clothes are ragged and no one really
wants us except for what we can do for them.
Yet despite our condition, the Master takes us
in His lap and cleans us up. He charges us
nothing and gives us everything. He performs
the miracle of healing the soul so that it can
see the inner light and he nurses us through
our recovery as the soul grows strong. Then
He takes us back to our Home.*

When we look into a true mystic's eyes and know
that this immaculate being, the Lord himself in
human form, actually loves us, even as we are,
then our sorrows just melt away in the fire of
his love.

Great Master Sawan Singh tells us:

*The maker of a lover is the Beloved, and it
is the internal attraction of the Beloved that
creates love. It is through his grace that love
remains alive.... The attitude of the disciple
towards his Master and God should be like
that of a moth for the flame, and he should
burn in the fire of his love for him.... The
lovers that forget themselves completely in
love for their Master drink from the fountain
of the Elixir of Life and attain eternal bliss.*

The mystics offer us the ways and means to attain God-realization. If we have a sincere desire to meet the Beloved, rest assured, they tell us, He will come. We simply need to open our hearts and ask for guidance.

Kabir, why need I worry, what can my worrying achieve? My Lord feels concern for me, I have no worries of my own. Do not be anxious, cast away your cares, the Beloved is all-powerful; do beasts, birds and insects have money in their pockets? The wish-fulfilling Jewel is ever present in your heart; dwell upon Him. Even if you do not worship Him, He constantly looks after you – for such is His wont.... Plow your field with the Lord's Name. Sow the seed of devotion; even if there is a drought 'til the end of the world, the seed will not fail to sprout nor fail to yield a rich crop.... What are you afraid of, O Kabir? The protecting hand of the Lord is always over your head.

Remember that wonderful poem, "The Touch of the Master's Hand"? Very descriptive of life and the struggles we face, and the role of the mystic who comes to free us, for he knows the worth of our soul:

'Twas battered, and scarred, and the auctioneer
Thought it scarcely worth his while
to waste much time on the old violin,
But he held it up with a smile.
"What am I bid, good folks?' He cried,
"who'll start the bidding for me?
A dollar, a dollar, now two, only two,
Two dollars and who'll make it three?
Three dollars once, three dollars twice
Going for three," but no!
From the room far back, a gray-haired man
Came forward and picked up the bow.
Then, wiping the dust from the old violin
And tightening up all the strings,
He played a melody pure and sweet,
As sweet as an angel sings.
The music ceased, and the auctioneer
with a voice that was quiet and low
Said, "What am I bid for the old violin?"
And he held it up with the bow.
"A thousand dollars, and who'll make it two?
Two thousand, and who'll make it three?
Three thousand once, three thousand twice,
and going and gone," said he.

The people cheered, but some of them cried,
"We do not quite understand.
What changed its worth?" Swift came the reply,
"The touch of the Master's Hand."
And many a man with life out of tune
and battered and torn with sin,
is auctioned cheap to a thoughtless crowd,
Much like the old violin.
A mess of pottage, a glass of wine,
A game, and he travels on.
He is going once, he is going twice,
He is going and almost gone.
But the Master comes, and the foolish crowd
Never can quite understand,
The worth of a soul, and the change that's wrought
By the Touch of the Master's Hand.

At this level, it is perhaps difficult to imagine the worth of our soul. We see and touch and sense everything through our human body, making choices based on the outer play of life.

The mystics often use the analogy of a needle and a magnet. The soul, unsullied by its karmic destiny, would fly straight back to the magnet. But because of its past actions done birth after birth in this creation, the soul is bound down and is held by the weight of the choices we have made.

However, the mystics show us the way to lighten our burden through meditation and prayer – and with sincere practice comes the gift of the Lord's grace. Hafiz states:

This is the kind of Friend You are – without making me realize my soul's anguished history, You slip into my house at night and while I am sleeping, You silently carry off all my suffering and sordid past in Your beautiful Hands.

What a blessing it is to recognize that God loves us and that we are part of the One – the divine being that brings light into every corner and every particle of creation.

The saints tell us our main job is to take action and turn inward toward the source. Love is an action word. There are many pathways that will lead to the Beloved's door. The mystics teach that when we search honestly and earnestly He will lead us to the one true way that is right for our soul. Tulsi Sahab says:

Cleanse the chamber of your heart for the coming of the Beloved. From your attention, discard all that is other, so that He may be seated there.

The saints emphasize that the path we choose to unlock the inner doors and windows will require action and attention and our earnest desire to step into the light. It is a path of stillness, an inner quiet that allows us to reflect and simply be more aware. Richard Rolle explains:

The soul is made wise by rest or sitting.... If he is not in the true quietness it follows he is not in true mindfulness. In what state may men love God the most? I answer in such state that they are most in rest of body and soul and least occupied with any needs or business of the world.... I know that I loved God more and longer-lastingly within the comfortableness of love. For sitting I am most in rest and my heart most upwards....

Contemplation (meditation) is sweet and desirable labour. It gladdens the labourer and hurts not. No man can do this and not feel joyful.... Nothing is more profitable, nothing sweeter, than the grace of meditation that lifts us from all low things and offers us to God...

*truly to know God; to love Him perfectly, and
in the shining of his majesty to see Him, and
with a wonderful song of joy and melody, to
praise Him without end.*

Run as fast as you can to his heart – that flame
which consumes, caresses and awakens the
sleeping soul to true consciousness and light
within. Run, my friend, for his door is wide open –
beckoning, beseeching, lighting the way to his lap.
Run, O Run for now is the moment – now is the
breath that has been granted to you. Savour this
invitation from the Beloved – act with haste – be
earnest and steadfast. This is your gift from the
Lord, your true heritage.

Hazur Maharaj Charan Singh lovingly tells us:

*We must not only hear the teachings – we
must engrave the teachings on our heart...
your Master is within you. He is always
watching you, whether you are conscious
about it or not. You can't escape His eyes.*

Those loving eyes that see all and understand all,
to the very depths of our soul. The saints teach
that the Lord is there for us in every breath, for
every step we take in life. The more we open our

hearts to his presence, the more we will feel his presence in each moment.

Contentment will grow, along with courage, conviction, trust, gratitude, acceptance, and love in its true form. What an incredible journey.

17

Only God remains

Rumi says:

*Love is a flame that, when kindled, burns
everything away – only God remains.*

Now the soul becomes immersed in the one, with
one-pointed attention at his feet within.

What remains to talk about? Only God. The saints
tell us that for the heart, there is nothing now but
the reality of his light and the sweetness of his
presence. Everything else becomes a shadow-
show. The richness and depth of his love will fill
us completely. We are with the Friend now and
the soul is singing. ...Nothing changes us like love.
Kabir tells us:

*When the Day came,
The Day I had lived and died for –*

The Day that is not in any calendar –
Clouds heavy with love
Showered me with wild abundance.
Inside me, my soul was drenched.
Around me, even the desert grew green.

The mystics say we never know when the Beloved will fill us completely with his love. As awareness grows within, we realize if our cup is turned up toward the light, his grace could pull us inwards and upwards in an instant. A glance from him could shatter all outer illusions and open us fully to the reality that we are soul. Lover and Beloved become entwined and only love's sweetness remains.

Sadi shares this story with us:

A young man who loved God turned his face
towards the desert. His father, grieved at his
absence, could not eat or sleep. A friend of
the family railed at the son for his behavior.
He could only reply, "My Friend has claimed
me as His own; now I can own no other
friendship but His. When He unveiled His
beauty to me, everything else I saw seemed
unreal." Those who love Him cannot care for
anyone else; their senses are shut away and

*bewildered in adoration, their ears are deaf to
any reproach.*

*Without a caravan, they wander through the
desert of divine knowledge. They have no
hope of understanding or approval from their
fellows, for they are the chosen of the elect of
God.*

The mystics tell us this is the secret – we are the
chosen ones of God, and the restlessness and
longing that we feel turn us in the only direction
our soul wishes to face: that of stepping into the
light.

Rumi says:

*From deep within my heart I always catch
the scent of my Beloved. How can I help but
follow that fragrance?*

The soul drop that we are begins to merge into
the vast ocean of his love. The saints say we will
start looking for him in all of our moments, and
the longing to know the truth will grow and grow.

Our attention shifts from the outer to the inner
and we take delight in the unfolding of our destiny.
By the grace of the saints and mystics we strive

to work hard to reclaim the richest treasure of all – our spiritual heritage.

As Kabir relates:

I went looking for Him
And lost myself;
The drop merged with the Sea –
Who can find it now?
Looking and looking for Him
I lost myself.
The Sea merged with the drop –
Who can find it now?

The mystics say when we follow the fragrance, take the steps, partake in the journey and knock on the door of love, we become fully conscious and present in each of our moments. Rumi speaks of this awakening:

I knocked on the door
Of the One who embraces Love.
He opened it, saw me there,
and began to laugh.
He pulled me in –
I melted like sugar cubes

In the Arms of that lover,
the Wizard of the World.

The mystics tell us that when all of our thoughts
are turned inward toward the Beloved, thoughts of
'I' and 'mine' cease to exist and there is only him,
the Beloved. As we smell his fragrance and hear
his voice, his Word becomes our very being and
we start seeing him everywhere and in everything.

Rumi says:

Here He comes – a moon whose light the sky
never saw even in her dreams. Crowned with
an eternal flame no flood can hope to quench.
His cup, long out of reach, now spills over,
filling my senses, desolating my soul.

The Saaqi has become my dearest friend.
With each new round she pours, my blood
turns to nectar, my heart to a holy shrine.
Now I see only HIM. Now I hear His voice
alone: Let my love fill your golden cup like
sunbeams showering the earth. Let it flow
to every corner of your soul, let it tear up the
gnarled roots of regret and nourish the tender
seeds of hope.

When my heart saw the ocean of His Love, it
jumped in and yelled, 'Find me if you can!'
O, where can I look for my missing heart?
Where, but the face of Shams-e-Tabriz?
(Rumi's spiritual teacher). He is the sun in
whose track every heart must follow.

The mystics say the ultimate for each and every soul is to be totally lost in the depths of the Beloved, to merge into the light completely.

Saint John of the Cross expresses this beautifully when he says:

On a dark night, inflamed by love and longing
(O exquisite adventure!) undetected I slipped
away. My house, at last, grew still. Secure in
the darkness, I climbed the secret ladder in
disguise, with no other light or guide than
the one burning in my heart. This light led
the way more clearly than the rising sun, to
where He was waiting for me, the one I
knew so intimately, in a place where no one
could find us. O night that guided me! O night
sweeter than sunrise! O night that joined lover
with Beloved, lover transformed in Beloved!

The saints promise this is the soul's reality, the true circle of love: being embraced by the divine and stepping into the light of our being. The journey of the soul ends with love – with **knowing** the Beloved is always there for us in every situation and that our soul is being continually drenched in the nectar of his Love.

To explore, expand and become one with the light is the true gift from the Beloved. Reach out and grasp the essence, my friends, for this treasure is for you.

Thank you.

What if possibilities

In the beginning of this book, we asked six questions to whet the appetite and explore the possibilities. So let's take them one by one and see where the answers may lead.

1. **What if there is a God – how do I reach Him/Her?**

For every seeker of the truth this question is paramount. Part of us is afraid of the answer – if there is a God, will we find a way to realize the truth while living in this human body? Weighty thoughts. Let us suppose that God does indeed exist. We can look throughout history and be reassured of God's ever presence in our lives. God is not a theory – He is real and a part of our every breath. Christ called it the Word, eastern mystics call it the Shabd or Audible Life Stream. This is the life force that gives breath to all living beings, and without it we would return to dust. Once we can accept that God is a reality in our lives, then we can take steps to seek the truth.

2. What if I have to give up more than I'm willing to give?

Well, we won't know until we explore the possibilities and see just what we need to do to become God-realized souls. Our life span is determined by our destiny at birth. The relationship between the soul and God is personal, and we want to give this experience every possible benefit to see what is real and true for us. Then, and only then, can we decide what is the right path for us.

3. What if I can't figure out whether the struggle is worth it?

There will be some days and moments where the struggle may seem too great to deal with. But with the strength and grace of the Lord, these moments will be overcome and replaced with a feeling of 'Yes! This is where I want to be and what I want and need to do with my life.' The Lord never gives a seeker more than he or she can handle. And the love from the Beloved is with us every step of the way. We can venture forth with confidence that the struggle will definitely be worth it for our soul.

4. **What if all my friends think I'm flaky?**

This is a definite possibility. Not everyone understands the need to search for the truth, and what it entails. Therefore they become uncomfortable and distant. True friends will try to see what is important to you and will be there whether they understand what you are seeking or not. This is a relationship between you and God, so it can be very private and personal as you go through life's daily routine. No one has to know unless you choose to tell them. However, your habits will change and people will notice. Always be aware of what is necessary for you – after all, this life has been gifted to you by the Creator, and we need to make a thorough study to make the best use of our time here.

5. **What if I don't ever find out?**

Scary! But rest assured, when you seek, you will find the answers. The Creator loves you and will not leave you in limbo. We simply need to knock, and knock some more, read and read some more, and when the mystic teachings are revealed to you, all of your questions will be answered and you will start the journey to God-realization.

6. **What if I actually achieve God-realization – what then?**

Then your soul will shine and become one with that divine creative power, the Shabd or Word. All will be realized and you will be blessed in the court of the Lord forever, having achieved the purpose of human life. Even while still in this human body, you will feel the Oneness and your remembrance will be complete.

Wow. Congratulations!

Notes on quotes, poems and stories

1: A PEEP INSIDE

The sun's eyes are painting fields   Hafiz; Daniel Ladinsky, *The Gift*.

The Lord is in me   Kabir; Andrew Harvey and Eryk Hanut, *Perfume of the Desert*.

No one can find the way to Him   Maghribi; Andrew Harvey and Eryk Hanut, *Perfume of the Desert*.

2: AWAKENING

Man's five senses are like five doors   Al-Ghazali; cited in Lekh Raj Puri, preface to *Mysticism, The Spiritual Path*.

Off and on, in some rare moments   S. Radhakrishnan.

I saw God on the streets Ruzbihan Baqli; Andrew Harvey and Eryk Hanut, *Perfume of the Desert.*

Don't speak of your suffering Sanai; Andrew Harvey and Eryk Hanut, *Perfume of the Desert.*

The fruit of love Mother Teresa.

O God, give me Light The Prophet; Andrew Harvey and Eyrk Hanut, *Perfume of the Desert.*

I do not want to step Hafiz; Daniel Ladinsky, *The Gift.*

Each moment from all sides Rumi; Andrew Harvey and Eyrk Hanut, *Perfume of the Desert.*

My Beloved said Hafiz; Daniel Ladinsky, *A Year with Hafiz.*

3: OPPORTUNITY KNOCKS

Picture the face of your Beloved Hafiz; Daniel Ladinsky, *A Year with Hafiz.*

If I dare to hear you Mark Nepo, *The Exquisite Risk.*

The abundance of life   Charles Fillmore; Mark Nepo, *The Exquisite Risk*.

We can keep beginning   Mark Nepo, *The Exquisite Risk*.

Come, come, whoever you are   Rumi; Andrew Harvey and Eyrk Hanut, *Perfume of the Desert*.

Where you stumble and fall   Joseph Campbell; Mark Nepo, *The Exquisite Risk*.

We have no concept of the soul   Maharaj Charan Singh, *The Master Answers*.

You see, we've always been on a journey   Mark Nepo, *The Exquisite Risk*.

4: THE PURPOSE OF HUMAN BIRTH

As to intellect   Maharaj Charan Singh, *Divine Light*.

You are more precious   Rumi.

Love alone is eternal   Maharaj Charan Singh, *Words Eternal*.

If you are kind Based on Kent Keith, "Paradoxical Commandments" – the modified version in Calcutta is often attributed to Mother Teresa.

Man seeks God Maharaj Charan Singh, *Quest for Light.*

5: WHAT IS REAL?

"A Thousand Mirrors" Swami Chidvilasananda.

There is a voice in all Rumi.

6: WHY ME?

How many times Hafiz; Daniel Ladinsky, *A Year with Hafiz.*

O my soul Rumi.

Life does not begin with birth Maharaj Charan Singh, *Words Eternal.*

You see, Master is a medium Maharaj Charan Singh, *Spiritual Perspectives.*

NOTES ON QUOTES, POEMS AND STORIES

Not many teachers in this world   Hafiz; Daniel Ladinsky, *The Gift*.

Rouse the eternal flames   Yogananda.

If we give ourselves   Maharaj Charan Singh, *Spiritual Heritage*.

A raindrop fell from a spring cloud   Sadi; Andrew Harvey and Eyrk Hanut, *Perfume of the Desert*.

The exquisite risk   Saint John of the Cross; Mark Nepo, *The Exquisite Risk*.

Be still and know   The Bible, Psalm 46:10.

Man is essentially divine   Maharaj Charan Singh, *Spiritual Discourses*.

The story of love   Kabir; Andrew Harvey and Eryk Hanut, *Perfume of the Desert*; also V.K. Sethi, *Kabir, The Weaver of God's Name*.

Birds initially had no desire   Hafiz; Daniel Ladinsky, *The Gift*.

7: THE WORD OF GOD

He (God) cannot be conceived　Richard Rolle.

Ceaselessly repeat the Name　Samarth Ramdas;
Judith Sankarnarayan, *Many Voices, One Song.*

Through the stairway of existence　Hafiz,
Daniel Ladinsky, *A Year with Hafiz.*

Nam, the priceless treasure of the Word
Maharaj Charan Singh, *Spiritual Discourses 1.*

8: DESTINY

As my sister and I prepared　Story in *Spiritual Link* magazine, July 2014.

What is Destiny?　Maharaj Charan Singh,
Spiritual Perspectives, Vol. 1.

Whatever we have sown　Maharaj Charan Singh,
Spiritual Perspectives, Vol. 1.

There is nothing to feel disheartened about
Great Master Sawan Singh, *Spiritual Gems.*

9: ACCEPTANCE AND TRUST

Those who accept his Word   Soami Shiv Dayal Singh Ji, *Sar Bachan Poetry*.

There were many prisoners   Great Master Sawan Singh as related by Hazur Maharaj Charan Singh, *Spiritual Perspectives*.

Then afterwards, during the question period Nancy Pope Mayorga, *Hunger of the Soul, A Spiritual Diary*.

The one who brings the soul   Hazur Maharaj Charan Singh, *Spiritual Discourses 1*.

If one wishes to become fearless   Great Master Sawan Singh, *Philosophy of the Masters, Vol. 3*.

Kabir, after careful thought   Kabir, source unknown.

If one thinks of the way things work   *Spiritual Link* magazine, "The Power of Love," August 2014.

Most people spend their entire lives   Eckhart Tolle, *Stillness Speaks,* cited in *Spiritual Link* magazine, August 2014.

10: WHO ARE WE?

In spite of our eyes   Hazur Maharaj Charan Singh, *Divine Light.*

The path to awakening   Thomas Merton.

God is in everything   Hazur Maharaj Charan Singh, *Spiritual Perspectives.*

The man in whom the Word of God   Hazur Maharaj Charan Singh, *Spiritual Perspectives.*

Why is a Master   Hazur Maharaj Charan Singh, Question and Answer session at Dera Baba Jaimal Singh, Punjab, India.

At the dining table   Sarmad; Isaac A. Ezekiel, *Sarmad, Martyr to Love Divine.*

The Word is the ocean   Mikhail Naimy, *Book of Mirdad.*

Life does not begin   Hazur Maharaj Charan Singh, *Quest for Light.*

The greatest romance   Yogananda, *Autobiography of a Yogi.*

I have enshrined   Soami Shiv Dayal Singh Ji, *Sar Bachan Poetry.*

An emperor had a slave   Andrew Harvey and Eryk Hanut, *Perfume of the Desert.*

What wouldn't I and hundreds   Shraddha Liertz, *Adventure of Faith.*

My mind is restless   Guru Ram Das, Adi Granth.

Please remember that great things   Hazur Maharaj Charan Singh, *Quest for Light.*

11: RENEWAL

When intense love is awakened   Great Master Sawan Singh, *My Submission.*

12: PRACTICING THE PRESENCE

In the beginning   Great Master Sawan Singh, *Philosophy of the Masters,* Abridged.

If after being born   Baba Jaimal Singh, *Spiritual Letters.*

It is one flash   Meister Eckhart.

The Master stills the mind   Great Master Sawan Singh, *Philosophy of the Masters*, vol.5.

Remember the deep root   Rumi; Coleman Barks, *The Soul of Rumi*.

It is the burning of the heart   Rumi, *Mathnavi*.

I wish I could show you   Hafiz; Daniel Ladinsky, *I Heard God Laughing*.

13: THE MAGIC OF A MYSTIC

O weary heart   Rumi; Jonathan Star, *In the Arms of the Beloved*.

Your face is towards the light   Great Master Sawan Singh, *Spiritual Gems*.

Life created out of intense love   Mansur.

136

14: PRACTICE MAKES PERFECT

Spirituality really is a very simple thing
Source unknown at time of printing.

The real meaning of satsang   Hazur Maharaj
Charan Singh, *Spiritual Perspectives.*

In order to pray correctly   Great Master Sawan
Singh, *Philosophy of the Masters,* vol.3.

The time of meditation   Shraddha Liertz,
Adventure of Faith.

15: THE GIFT OF HIS GRACE

In life's experience   Sarmad; Isaac A. Ezekiel,
Sarmad, Martyr to Love Divine.

If you take one step   Bhai Gurdas Ji.

In the beginning we have to make an effort
Brother Lawrence, *The Practice of the Presence
of God.*

The earth and sky will open your purse   Rumi.

I have filled my disciples   Hazur Maharaj Charan Singh, commenting on the Gospel of St John in *Light on Saint John.*

16: FULFILLMENT

It is your destiny   Rumi.

When an overwhelming adversity   "Sukhmani," Guru Arjan, Adi Granth, cited in Maharaj Sawan Singh, *Philosophy of the Masters,* vol.1.

In the morning   Hafiz; Daniel Ladinsky, *I heard God Laughing.*

When the Master finds us   *RS Greetings Magazine,* Winter, 1994.

The maker of a lover   Great Master Sawan Singh, *Philosophy of the Masters,* vol.2.

Kabir, why need I worry   Kabir.

'Twas battered and scarred   Myra Brooks Welch, "The Touch of the Master's Hand."

This is the kind of friend   Hafiz; Daniel Ladinsky, *The Gift.*

Cleanse the chamber of your heart   Tulsi Sahib, *Tulsi Sahib, Saint of Hathras.*

The soul is made wise   Richard Rolle, *Science of the Soul Magazine.*

We must not only hear   Hazur Maharaj Charan Singh, evening meeting at Dera Baba Jaimal Singh, Punjab.

17: ONLY GOD REMAINS

Love is that flame   Rumi.

When the day came   Kabir; Andrew Harvey and Eryk Hanut, *Perfume of the Desert.*

A young man who loved God   Sadi; Andrew Harvey and Eryk Hanut, *Perfume of the Desert.*

From deep within my heart   Rumi; Jonathan Star, *In the Arms of the Beloved.*

I went looking for him Kabir; Andrew Harvey and Eryk Hanut, *Perfume of the Desert.*

I knocked on the door Rumi; Jonathan Star, *In the Arms of the Beloved.*

Here he comes Rumi; Jonathan Star, *In the Arms of the Beloved.*

On a dark night Saint John of the Cross; *Dark Night of the Soul.* Anthea Guinness, The Inner Way.

A thankful heart

This book has unfolded due to the grace and love of my Satguru, Hazur Maharaj Charan Singh and His successor, Baba Gurinder Singh. I can only lay the pages of the written word at their feet, thanking them for each thought and each breath of remembrance.

For all seekers of truth and spirituality, may something that is shared in these pages touch your heart with the desire to know and understand what stepping into the light of your being means to your soul.

Grateful acknowledgements

I am grateful to all of my spiritual family, who have helped bring this manuscript to you:

Cynthia Spring for her incredible artwork for the cover.

Anthea Guinness at Salt River Publishing for her patience, advice and help in so many ways to shape the final document and publish it.

Peter Korzaan, my husband, who was encouraging at every step.

And all of my friends who gave such a positive response to the idea of this book.

A heartfelt THANK YOU to everyone.

Warm wishes,

Gretchen xxoo

Appreciation

*T*hank you for buying
a copy of this Salt River book.

And thanks for telling your friends
to do so, too – the authors appreciate your help
getting the word out.

If you would like to help further,
we would love you to leave a comment
at Amazon, sharing your response
to any of the SRP books.

Available at Amazon.com
Discount at SaltRiverPublishing.com

[handwritten: ✓ revised version]

Salt River Booklist

Global Library Books

- Janice Fletcher, EdD – *Teach with Spirit: A teacher's inward journey guide*
- Anthea Guinness – *The inner way: A mystic anthology of songpoems, stories, reflections*
- Anthea Guinness – *Wake up! if you can: Sayings of Kabir with reflections and mystic stories*
- Anthea Guinness – *A path of love: Talks with Soami Ji of Agra* – BOOK 1 *K
- Anthea Guinness – *Becoming a disciple: Talks with Soami Ji of Agra* – BOOK 2 *K
- Anthea Guinness – *Hidden treasure: Spiritual poems by Soami Ji of Agra* – BOOK 3 *K

Tuppany Books

- Shanan Harrell – *Stumbling towards enlightenment* *K
- Gretchen Korzaan – *Stepping into the light*
- Renata Mongillo – *Figure it out*
- Rosemary Rawson – *Coming of age* *K
- Elley-Ray Tsipolitis – *Butterfly kisses*
- Elley-Ray Tsipolitis – *Fly with eagles*

Pocketbooks

- Anthea Guinness – *Dawn has come: Songpoems of Paltu*

Beyond Borders Books
- Dyan Dubois – *Rajasthan suite memory* – a novel *K

New Moon Books for children
- Gretchen Korzaan – *Runt, the littlest donkey*
- Tia Pleiman, Village Voices series – *I am the rainbow, With my hands, Color in the book, In my dreams*

Eye of an Artist Books
- Greg Meyer – *Arizona places: Otherworldly and beautiful*
- Janis White – *A widow's journey: An odyssey of healing*

Independent Publications Salt River assistance with editing – and/or book design, composition, cover design
- Rosemary Rawson – *Dark bread and dancing*
- Farida Sharan – *Dance with cancer*
- Chloe Faith Wordsworth – *Living in Tune* series, *Quantum change, Spiral up!* and all the Resonance Repatterning books

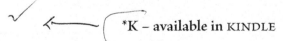

www.SaltRiverPublishing.com

*K – available in KINDLE

Colophon

Typefaces: Bookmania (designed by Mark Simonson), Philosopher (designed by Jovanny Lemonad), Adobe Brioso Pro (designed by Robert Slimbach)
Software: Adobe InDesign
Book Design: Anthea Guinness of Salt River Publishing
Composition: Anthea Guinness
Cover Art, used with permission: Cynthia Spring
Cover Design: Cynthia Spring
Printer: KDP.com
Printing method: Print-on-Demand (POD) digital
Paper: Library quality

SR

www.SaltRiverPublishing.com

Salt River

Salt River Publishing believes in encouraging artists and publishing professionals to come together and reach their empowered "Yes!"

Salt River was established as a no-profit publisher
- to help writers, translators, poets, graphic artists and photographers bring their work into publishable form and make 100% of the profit on their book sales
- and to promote, for free, the expertise of publishing professionals whose services an author might need when they have a book in the making

We publish books that inspire, encourage or entertain, including children's books – and books that deepen the understanding of mysticism.

Do you have one?

SR

www.SaltRiverPublishing.com

Reader response
to Salt River books

"So many problems are spiritual in nature. And healing often involves finding meaning, purpose and spiritual uplift. The right words at the right time can turn a life around. Therapists and practitioners can point the way for clients who are seeking meaning; writers and artists have an opportunity to share in that work. Thank you, Salt River."

V, 108-109

p75 omit dates — only time dates are given!

120 John of Cross ... no ref + incomplete (line missing in middle)
see IV 167

Made in the USA
Monee, IL
05 September 2020